Math Connections

Activities for Grades 4–6

David J. Glatzer

Joyce Glatzer

DALE SEYMOUR PUBLICATIONS

Managing Editor: Michael Kane
Project Editor: Katarina Stenstedt
Production Manager: Janet Yearian
Production Coordinator: Leanne Collins
Design Manager: Jeff Kelly
Text Design: Detta Penna

Dale Seymour Publications is an imprint of Addison-Wesley Publishing.

 **DALE
SEYMOUR
PUBLICATIONS**
P.O. Box 10888
Palo Alto, CA. 94303

 This book is printed
on recycled paper.

ISBN 0-86651-634-4
Order number DS21205

3 4 5 6 7 8-ML-98 97 96 95

Contents

Introduction

Purpose

These blackline masters offer mathematics teachers a variety of nonroutine problem activities designed to encourage critical thinking within the context of the mathematics curriculum. The activities ask students to verbalize understandings and to contrast major mathematical ideas. Although the activities are intended for grades 4–6, each may be adapted to other grades. Similar volumes by the same authors, *Math Connections: Middle School Activities* and *Math Intersections,* have been developed for middle school students (Dale Seymour Publications, 1989 and 1990).

Philosophy

Consistent with the National Council of Teachers of Mathematics' *Curriculum and Evaluation Standards for School Mathematics,* activities at the intermediate level should foster communication, reasoning, and problem solving. The nonroutine activities in this book address higher levels of thinking, focus on concept development, and encourage communication and reasoning. As students use activities in this book, they will begin to function at higher levels of thinking and will increase their confidence regarding their ability to "talk" mathematics. These activities allow students to take ownership of their learning experience.

Organization

The book is organized in six sections, each with a different activity format. Each section contains problems from several content categories, such as numeration and number sense, operations, fractions, decimals, geometry, measurement, and patterns and relationships. The problems are arranged in order of difficulty.

Suggested answers are provided in the Answer Section of this book, although for many problems the students may come up with other acceptable solutions or rationales. As a model, the first problem on each page is answered for the student.

Each section contains an introduction that explains the nature of the activities in that section, works through sample problems, and describes the section's follow-up problems.

Each page in a section concludes with a follow-up question called Completing the Connection. These questions help you assess the students' overall understanding and help the students reach closure.

Use of the Material

There is no one way to use this book. It can be adapted to the needs of your students. However, they will receive the greatest benefit if you provide opportunities for them to share the thought processes they used in arriving at their answers.

- Classroom discussion—Make a photocopy of the page for each student and a transparency of the same page for yourself. Discuss the problems one at a time, encouraging the students to support their answers. You may decide to only use one or two questions for warm-up purposes at the start of a class period.

- Small-group work—Divide the students into small groups of three or four, and have each group devote time and effort to a thorough discussion of each problem. This approach may follow the model of cooperative learning groups.

- Use of manipulatives—Encourage students to use manipulatives to illustrate solutions or explore the questions more fully.

- Student-generated extensions—When the class finishes a page, ask the students to write additional problems of the same form.

Conclusion

Remember that the activities in this book
- can be used throughout the year
- can be used to provide variety in the math curriculum
- can be used to preview and review concepts
- can be used to increase student involvement
- are easily adaptable
- are open-ended and easily extended
- are fun

The ideas contained in this book have been used successfully in classrooms at the intermediate levels and in teacher in-service programs.

Math Connections

Section I

Which One Doesn't Belong?

Introduction

The **Which One Doesn't Belong?** activity format allows students to concentrate on the critical attributes associated with specific topics in mathematics. They are asked to determine how three of four given items are related. Recognition of relationships and patterns is fundamental for success in math. Furthermore, the ability to verbalize these relationships is necessary to ensure understanding. In stating the rationale for a response, the student must indicate the characteristic common to the three related items.

Sample Exercises

Study the four items in each row. Circle the item that does not belong. Be prepared to give a reason for your answer. There may be more than one correct answer.

	A	B	C	D
1.	30	40	(45) *The other three are multiples of 10.*	50
2.	$\dfrac{7}{5}$	$\left(\dfrac{4}{5}\right)$ *The other three are improper fractions.*	$\left(\dfrac{5}{3}\right)$ *The other three have denominators of 5.*	$\dfrac{6}{5}$

In each problem in this section, students are asked to examine the four items and select the oddball, the item that doesn't belong with the other three. For example, in problem 1 in the sample exercise, a possible answer is C, since the other three items are multiples of ten. However, since the directions are open-ended, it is possible that different students will come up with different answers for any given problem. For example, in problem 2 in the sample exercise, one possible answer is B, since the other three are improper fractions. Another possible answer is C, since the other three all have denominators of 5.

Note that in giving B as the answer for problem 2, students may reason that $\frac{4}{5}$ is a proper fraction. Although this is true, encourage students to also identify the property common to the three related items.

To assess students' understanding of this activity, the follow-up problem on each page asks students to create their own Which One Doesn't Belong? problem for a category provided. Although all the students are dealing with the same conditions, they will write different problems. It would be beneficial for them to share their ideas in a class discussion. For instance, in the Completing the Connection problem for "Numeration and Number Sense," students are asked to list four numbers, three that round to 50 and one that does not. Many sets of answers are possible:

51, 47, 55, 46
45, 46, 47, 44
54, 51, 46, 37, etc.

Numeration and Number Sense

Study the four items in each row. Circle the item that does not belong. Be prepared to give a reason for your answer. There may be more than one correct answer.

	A	B	C	D
1.	27	29	(34) *The other three numbers are odd.*	35
2.	28	30	31	32
3.	12	16	24	26
4.	5 tens 4 ones	4 tens 14 ones	4 tens 5 ones	54 ones
5.	tens	hundredths	thousands	hundreds
6.	29, 28, 27	21, 22, 23	34, 35, 36	47, 48, 49
7.	Number of days in October	Number of days in a year	Number of states in the U.S.	Number of letters in the alphabet
8.	78	79	82	87

> > > > > > > > > > > > **COMPLETING THE CONNECTION** < < < < < < < < < < < <

List four numbers. Three of the numbers round to 50.
One of the numbers does not round to 50.

Operations

Study the four items in each row. Circle the item that does not belong. Be prepared to give a reason for your answer. There may be more than one correct answer.

	A	B	C	D
1.	9 x 4	(2 x 16) *The other three have 36 as a product.*	3 x 12	6 x 6
2.	32 ÷ 4	5 + 3	17 − 8	4 x 2
3.	60 + 40	25 x 4	4732 − 3732	400 ÷ 4
4.	27 + 69	74 + 31	18 + 81	12 + 53
5.	453 − 443	692 − 682	814 − 804	837 − 834
6.	374 − 262	363 − 275	482 − 294	534 − 496
7.	625 ÷ 25	25$\overline{)625}$	$\dfrac{625}{25}$	25 ÷ 625
8.	7 x 8 x 5	14 x 5 x 2	7 x 4 x 5	35 x 2 x 2

> > > > > > > > > > > > **COMPLETING THE CONNECTION** < < < < < < < < < < < < <

List four multiplication problems. Three of the products have a 2 in the ones place.
One of the products does not have a 2 in the ones place.

Fractions and Decimals

Study the four items in each row. Circle the item that does not belong. Be prepared to give a reason for your answer. There may be more than one correct answer.

	A	B	C	D
1.	$\frac{1}{2}$	$\frac{2}{4}$	$\frac{3}{6}$	$\boxed{\frac{3}{9}}$ *The other three are equivalent to 1/2.*
2.	◺	●● ○○	◐	▨
3.	$\frac{3}{6}$	$\frac{3}{10}$	$\frac{3}{9}$	$\frac{3}{12}$
4.	$\frac{5}{10}$	$\frac{1}{2}$	0.5	$\frac{5}{100}$
5.	50 cents	6 inches	30 minutes	1 foot
6.	$\frac{7}{8}$	$\frac{5}{3}$	$\frac{3}{2}$	$\frac{7}{4}$
7.	$\frac{1}{4}, \frac{3}{4}$	$\frac{5}{6}, \frac{3}{6}$	$\frac{2}{3}, \frac{1}{3}$	$\frac{2}{5}, \frac{3}{5}$
8.	1.54	1.75	1.4	1.6

> > > > > > > > > > > > **COMPLETING THE CONNECTION** < < < < < < < < < < < <

List four fractions. Three of the fractions are between $\frac{1}{2}$ and 1. One of the fractions is not between $\frac{1}{2}$ and 1.

Geometry

Study the four items in each row. Circle the item that does not belong. Be prepared to give a reason for your answer. There may be more than one correct answer.

	A	B	C	D
1.	square	rectangle	(triangle) *The other three are four-sided figures.*	parallelogram
2.	cone	sphere	pyramid	square
3.	△	△	△	△
4.	∠	∠	∠	∠
5.	↔	↕	↕	✕
6.	⬠	⬠	⬠	⬠
7.	⊓	F	T	H
8.	B|ꓭ	V|∧	N|И	Z|Ƨ

> > > > > > > > > > > > **COMPLETING THE CONNECTION** < < < < < < < < < < < <

List the names of four polygons. Three are names of polygons that have four sides.
One is the name of a polygon that does not have four sides.

Measurement

Study the four items in each row. Circle the item that does not belong. Be prepared to give a reason for your answer. There may be more than one correct answer.

	A	B	C	D
1.	centimeter	meter	(gallon) *The other three are units of length.*	kilometer
2.	hour	second	minute	inch
3.	gallon	quart	pint	pound
4.	January	September	May	October
5.	31°F	65°F	85°F	43°F
6.	1 foot 6 inches	$\frac{1}{2}$ yard	18 inches	2 feet 1 inch
7.	3 △ 5, 4	4 □ 4, 4 4	2 ▭ 4	2 2⬡2 2, 2 2
8.	4 ▭ 9	6 ▭ 8	3 ▭ 12	2 ▭ 18

> > > > > > > > > > > > **COMPLETING THE CONNECTION** < < < < < < < < < < < < <

List four measures. Three are measures of weight. One
is not a measure of weight.

Which One Doesn't Belong?   **9**

Patterns and Relationships

Study the four items in each row. Circle the item that does not belong. Be prepared to give a reason for your answer. There may be more than one correct answer.

	A	B	C	D
1.	2, 4, 6 . . .	14, 16, 18 . . .	(3, 5, 7 . . .) *The other three are sequences of even numbers.*	0, 2, 4 . . .
2.	1, 3, 5 . . .	2, 4, 6 . . .	7, 9, 11 . . .	6, 9, 12 . . .
3.	13, 9, 5 . . .	10, 7, 4 . . .	15, 12, 9 . . .	6, 3, 0 . . .
4.	10, 20, 30 . . .	70, 80, 90 . . .	100, 110, 120 . . .	100, 200, 300 . . .
5.	1221	1212	2442	3553
6.	BOB	MOM	MOON	RADAR
7.	$\frac{3}{7}$	$\frac{1}{3}$	$\frac{3}{5}$	$\frac{5}{7}$
8.	0.12	0.49	0.24	0.36

> > > > > > > > > > > > **COMPLETING THE CONNECTION** < < < < < < < < < < < <

List four sequences. Three sequences have terms that differ by 5.
One sequence does not have terms that differ by 5.

Section 2

How Do You
Know That?

Introduction

The **How Do You Know That?** activity format gives students an opportunity to use words to express key concepts in mathematics. The ability to explain relationships is a better indicator of comprehension than the mechanical completion of standard computational examples. Therefore, this activity format focuses on relationships rather than computation. Cooperative learning and divergent thinking are encouraged, and students are challenged to demonstrate number sense.

For each question presented in this section, students are asked to write one or more complete sentences. Responses will vary. If students have difficulty writing their responses, responses could be given orally. In formulating responses, students should use their knowledge of definitions, relationships, and estimation skills.

Sample Exercises

Write one or more complete sentences to answer each question. Answers may vary.

1. How do you know that 6 is a factor of 42?

When 42 is divided by 6, the remainder is 0.

2. How do you know that 105 centimeters is longer than 1 meter?

One meter contains 100 centimeters, and 105 is greater than 100.

Remind students that diagrams can be part of their answers.

To summarize, the Completing the Connection question has students reflect on the concepts used to answer the questions in this section. Specifically, they are asked to write at least two things that they know about a given concept or situation. For example, in the Numeration and Number Sense section, a student may list the following characteristics about the number 124:

• It is greater than 100.
• It has a 1 in the hundreds place, 2 in the tens place, 4 in the ones place.
• It is less than 200.
• It is even.
• It is divisible by four.

Answers may vary. Student responses should be shared to increase recognition of attributes and properties.

Numeration and Number Sense

Write one or more complete sentences to answer each question. Answers may vary.

1. How do you know that 46 rounds to 50?

46 is between 40 and 50 but closer to 50.

2. How do you know that 453 > 435?

3. How do you know that four thousand six is not written 406?

4. How do you know that 46 is between 47 and 45?

5. How do you know that 54 is the same as 4 tens and 14 ones?

6. How do you know that 400 is a good estimate for 99 + 102 + 98 + 107?

7. How do you know that 4 is not a factor of 42?

8. How do you know that multiples of 5 must end in 5 or 0?

> > > > > > > > > > > **COMPLETING THE CONNECTION** < < < < < < < < < < <

Write at least two things that you know about 124.

Operations

Write one or more complete sentences to answer each question. Answers may vary.

1. How do you know that 453 − 257 < 200?

   Since 453 − 253 = 200 and 257 is greater than 253,
   the final difference must be less than 200.

2. How do you know that 5 + 5 + 5 is the same as 3 x 5?

3. How do you know that 17 − 25 < 0?

4. How do you know that 710 − 590 is not the same as 590 − 710?

5. How do you know that 236 ÷ 5 has a remainder of 1?

6. How do you know that 34 is not the quotient of 1216 ÷ 4?

7. How do you know that the product of 45 and 32 is between 1200 and 1500?

8. How do you know that 50 is not the average of 40, 48, and 49?

> > > > > > > > > > > > COMPLETING THE CONNECTION < < < < < < < < < < < <

Write at least two things that you know about 3 + 3 + 3 + 3.

Fractions and Decimals

Write one or more complete sentences to answer each question. Answers may vary.

1. How do you know that $\frac{4}{8}$ and $\frac{1}{2}$ are equivalent?

   4 out of 8 gives the same value as 1 out of 2.

2. How do you know that $\frac{1}{5} < \frac{1}{4}$?

3. How do you know that $\frac{7}{6} > 1$?

4. How do you know that $2\frac{1}{2} + 3\frac{2}{3} > 6$?

5. How do you know that $\frac{16}{25}$ is in lowest terms?

6. How do you know that $0.5 + 0.7 > 1$?

7. How do you know that $0.045 < 0.405$?

8. How do you know that $\frac{2}{5}$ is not equal to 2.5?

> > > > > > > > > > > > **COMPLETING THE CONNECTION** < < < < < < < < < < < <

Write at least two things that you know about $\frac{4}{8}$.

Geometry

Write one or more complete sentences to answer each question. Answers may vary.

1. How do you know that all quadrilaterals are not rectangles?

   Rectangles must have four right angles.
   Many quadrilaterals do not have right angles.

2. How do you know that a square is a rectangle?

3. How do you know that *ABC* is not an acute angle?

4. How do you know that all rectangles are not congruent?

5. How do you know that △*ABC* is congruent to △*DEF*?

   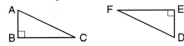

6. How do you know that the letter E has line symmetry?

7. How do you know that R changed to ꓤ did not result from a single reflection?

8. How do you know that the given imprint was not made by a cube?

   ◯

> > > > > > > > > > > > **COMPLETING THE CONNECTION** < < < < < < < < < < < < <

Write at least two things that you know about the following figure.

Measurement

Write one or more complete sentences to answer each question. Answers may vary.

1. How do you know that the area of the given triangle is less than the area of the given rectangle?

   The triangle is half of the rectangle.

2. How do you know that doubling the dimensions of a rectangle doubles the perimeter?

3. How do you know that doubling the dimensions of a rectangle more than doubles the area?

4. How do you know that 2 quarters, 1 dime, and 2 nickels equal 7 dimes?

5. How do you know that March 22nd is a Sunday if you know that March 14th is a Saturday?

6. How do you know that 400 cm is the same as 4 meters?

7. How do you know that 3 feet 6 inches is less than 48 inches?

8. How do you know that a month with 5 Mondays cannot have 5 Thursdays?

> > > > > > > > > > > > **COMPLETING THE CONNECTION** < < < < < < < < < < < <

Write at least two things that you know about the following figure.

2"

6"

Patterns and Relationships

Write one or more complete sentences to answer each question. Answers may vary.

1. How do you know that 14 is not in the sequence 0, 4, 8, 12 . . . ?

   Each term is found by adding 4 to the previous term.
   The next term would be 16, not 14.

2. How do you know that 30 is the tenth term in the sequence 3, 6, 9 . . . ?

3. How do you know that oc*tagon* is not the next term in the sequence *triangle, quadrilateral, pentagon, hexagon . . . ?*

4. How do you know that $\frac{9}{12}$ is not in the sequence $\frac{2}{3}, \frac{4}{6}, \frac{6}{9}$ . . . ?

5. How do you know that O is not in the twentieth place in the sequence TWOTWOTWOTWO . . . ?

6. How do you know that 1011 is not a palindrome?

7. How do you know that a negative number is the next term in the sequence 15, 10, 5, 0 . . . ?

8. How do you know that an odd number of tiles will be needed to build the fifteenth term of the pattern
   □, □□, □□□ . . . ?

> > > > > > > > > > > **COMPLETING THE CONNECTION** < < < < < < < < < < < <

Write at least two things that you know about the following pattern.
3, 6, 9, 12 . . .

Section 3

What If?

Introduction

The **What If?** activity format has students explore the impact of specific conditions or changes in the conditions of a situation. They are asked to determine what will happen in a variety of contexts as changes are indicated. This activity fosters the development of reasoning skills.

For each question in this section, the student is asked to write one or more complete sentences. In formulating responses, students are encouraged to examine specific examples or to draw diagrams that fit the condition and to use manipulatives to visualize the situation. Questions may be answered orally instead of in writing.

Sample Exercises

Write one or more complete sentences to answer each question.

1. What will happen to the average of 3 numbers if each number is increased by 5?

If each of the 3 numbers is increased by 5, the average increases by 5:
(3 + 4 + 8) ÷ 3 = 5
(8 + 9 + 13) ÷ 3 = 10

2. What will the sum be if 2 decimals, each in the tenths place, are added?

A student may think of an example such as 0.4 + 0.5 and respond, "The sum is in the tenths place." Another may think of an example such as 0.4 + 0.7 and respond, "The sum is greater than 1." Students should be encouraged to examine the situation for all possible cases.

To summarize, the Completing the Connection section asks students to select a vocabulary word found on the page and write or illustrate the definition of the word. For example, in the Operations section, a student may select the word quotient and give the definition "the answer to a division problem."

Numeration and Number Sense

Write a phrase or one or more complete sentences to answer each question.

1. What type of number results if an odd and even number are added?

   An odd number results:
   3 + 4 = 7
   21 + 26 = 47

2. What type of number results if an odd and even number are multiplied?

3. What is the number if the digit in the thousands place is 2 more than the digit in the hundreds place, the digit in the hundreds place is 3 less than the digit in the tens place, the digit in the tens place is 2 more than the digit in the ones place, and the digit in the ones place is 2?

4. What is the number of bundles of sticks needed to represent 1,000,000 if the sticks are grouped in 100s?

5. What number from the set 27, 39, 43, or 51 is not included if you count by 3s?

6. What are the different ways that peanuts can be shared equally if there are 36 peanuts and less than 10 people?

7. What is the largest 4-digit number you can write if the digits 4, 6, 5, and 9 are each used once?

8. What is the largest 3-digit number you can write that rounds to 300 if the digits 3, 5, 4, and 7 can be used?

> > > > > > > > > > > > **COMPLETING THE CONNECTION** < < < < < < < < < < < <

Select a mathematical term found on this page and write or illustrate its definition.

Operations

Write a phrase or one or more complete sentences to answer each question.

1. In an addition problem, what happens to the sum if 5 is added to one addend and subtracted from another addend?
   The sum stays the same.

2. In an addition problem, what happens to the sum if each addend in the problem is multiplied by 2?

3. In a subtraction problem, what happens to the difference if 5 is added to the minuend and subtracted from the subtrahend?

4. In a multiplication problem, what happens to the product if each factor is multiplied by 2?

5. In a multiplication problem, what happens to the product if one factor is doubled and the other is divided by 2?

6. In a division problem, what happens to the quotient if the divisor and dividend are both multiplied by 2?

7. In a division problem, what happens to the quotient if the dividend is multiplied by 2 and the divisor is divided by 2?

8. In a multiplication problem, what happens to the product if 1 is added to each factor?

> > > > > > > > > > > > **COMPLETING THE CONNECTION** < < < < < < < < < < < < <

Select a mathematical term found on this page and write or illustrate its definition.

Fractions and Decimals

Write a phrase or one or more complete sentences to answer each question.

1. What is the value of the fraction if the numerator and denominator are equal?

   The value of the fraction is 1.

2. What happens to the value of the fraction if the numerator and denominator are both doubled?

3. What happens to the value of the fraction if the denominator of the fraction is made larger?

4. What is the value of the fraction if the numerator is greater than the denominator?

5. What happens to the value of the fraction if the numerator is increased by 1?

6. What happens to the value of the fraction if the denominator is decreased by 1?

7. What happens to the value of a number if the decimal point is moved one place to the left?

8. What happens to the value of a number if the decimal point is moved two places to the right?

> > > > > > > > > > > **COMPLETING THE CONNECTION** < < < < < < < < < < < <

Select a mathematical term found on this page and write or illustrate its definition.

Geometry

Write a phrase or one or more complete sentences to answer each question.

1. What shapes are formed if a rectangle is cut in half?

   The shapes could be two rectangles, two squares, or two right triangles.

2. What is formed if an obtuse angle is cut in half?

3. What shape is formed if you place two squares next to each other?

4. What should be done to ⬆ if you want it to look like ➡ ?

5. What is true about a figure if the left half of the figure is congruent to the right half?

6. What shape is formed if a rectangle is spun on its height?

7. What shape is formed if the label is unwrapped from a cylindrical can?

8. What is the shape of the cut-off piece if you cut a corner off a cube?

> > > > > > > > > > > > **COMPLETING THE CONNECTION** < < < < < < < < < < < <

Select a mathematical term found on this page and write or illustrate its definition.

Measurement

Write a phrase or one or more complete sentences to answer each question.

1. For a given rectangle, what happens to the perimeter if you double the length and width?

   If you double the length and width, the perimeter is also doubled.

2. For a given rectangle, what happens to the area if you double the length and width?

3. For a given rectangle, what happens to the area if you double the length and cut the width in half?

4. For a given rectangular solid, what happens to the volume if you double the length, width, and height?

5. What do you know about a given month if the first of the month that follows it falls on the same day of the week as the first of the given month?

6. What day of the week will New Year's Eve be on if the previous New Year's Eve was on a Wednesday and there is a leap year?

7. What will the temperature be in 4 hours if it is currently 57°F and is dropping 5° each hour?

8. What time is it if the sum of the digits showing the time on a digital clock is 23?

> > > > > > > > > > > > **COMPLETING THE CONNECTION** < < < < < < < < < < < <

Select a mathematical term found on this page and write or illustrate its definition.

Patterns and Relationships

Write a phrase or one or more complete sentences to answer each question.

1. What are the next 5 terms in the sequence if the first 6 are 4, 7, 11, 16, 22, and 29?

    You would add 8 to get the next term, then 9, and so forth.
    The next 5 terms would be 37, 46, 56, 67, and 79.

2. What are the next 5 terms in a sequence if the first 2 are 5 and 10 and each term after 10 is the sum of the 2 terms before it?

3. What color would be in the thirtieth term of the sequence if the sequence is red, blue, green, red, blue, green, red, blue, green . . . ?

4. What is the direction of the arrow in the twenty-fourth term of the sequence if the sequence is →, ↑, ↓, ←, →, ↑, ↓, ← . . . ?

5. What would happen to the pattern 3, 6, 9, 12 . . . if you added 2 to each term in the sequence?

6. What is the sum of 10, 20, 30, 40, 50, 60 if the sum of 1, 2, 3, 4, 5, 6 is 21?

7. What is the number of square tiles that need to be added to make a square one size larger if the first square is made with 4 square tiles?

8. What are the next 5 terms in the sequence if the first 4 are 25, 20, 15, 10 . . . ?

> > > > > > > > > > > **COMPLETING THE CONNECTION** < < < < < < < < < < <

Select a mathematical term found on this page and write or illustrate its definition.

Section 4

Same and Different

Introduction

The **Same and Different** activity format provides students with the opportunity to explore the attributes of a given pair of items. Students are expected to analyze each member of the given pair to determine at least one way in which the items are the same and at least one way in which the items are different. Students should be encouraged to list as many common and different attributes of the pair as they can. The activity requires a good sense of numbers, relationships, properties, definitions, and patterns. While the activity requires the use of knowledge and comprehension levels of thinking, students are also using higher levels such as analysis and synthesis.

Sample Exercises

For each pair, state at least one way in which the items are the same and at least one way in which the items are different. List as many similarities and differences as you can.

1. June versus July

Same

- *both are months of the year*
- *both are summer months*

Different

- *July has 31 days and June has 30*
- *June is school month and July is not*

2. 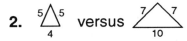 versus

Same

- *both are triangles*
- *both have two sides with equal measure*

Different

- *one has an obtuse angle*
- *perimeters are different*

To assess the students' understanding of this activity, a follow-up question on each page has been included. In it students are asked to complete a mathematical analogy. Besides serving as an assessment tool, the Completing the Connection question provides students with the opportunity to summarize the concepts learned in this activity and attain closure. In the Measurement section, students are asked to complete the analogy, length : meter as weight : _____. It is expected that students will identify the relationship linking length to meter and establish a similar relationship linking weight to *gram*.

Numeration and Number Sense

For each pair, state at least one way in which the items are the same and at least one way in which the items are different. List as many similarities and differences as you can.

1. 357 versus 457

Same

- *three-digit numbers*
- *odd numbers*
- *5 tens and 7 ones*

Different

- *one is less than 400 and one is greater than 400*
- *357 contains only odd digits and 457 contains one even digit*

2. 24 versus 36

Same

Different

3. 18 versus 19

Same

Different

4. billion versus million

Same

Different

5. 54 versus 4 tens 14 ones

Same

Different

6. 15 versus XV

Same

Different

> > > > > > > > > > > > **COMPLETING THE CONNECTION** < < < < < < < < < < < <

Complete the following analogy so that the relationship between the second pair is the same as the relationship between the first pair. 10 x 10 : hundred as 10 x 10 x 10 : _____

Operations

For each pair, state at least one way in which the items are the same and at least one way in which the items are different. List as many similarities and differences as you can.

1. 3 + 3 + 3 versus 3 x 3

Same

- *both number sentences equal 9*
- *both represent three groups of 3*

Different

- *one is addition and one is multiplication*

2. 161 + 349 versus 202 + 297

Same

Different

3. 9 + 7 = 16 versus 16 − 7 = 9

Same

Different

4. 4)‾40‾   versus 4)‾400‾

Same

Different

5. 27 ÷ 4 versus 33 ÷ 5

Same

Different

6. average of 10, 20, 30 versus average of 10, 20, 20, 30

Same

Different

> > > > > > > > > > > **COMPLETING THE CONNECTION** < < < < < < < < < < < <

Complete the following analogy so that the relationship between the second pair is the same as the relationship between the first pair. sum : addition as difference : _____

Fractions and Decimals

For each pair, state at least one way in which the items are the same and at least one way in which the items are different. List as many similarities and differences as you can.

1. $\frac{1}{4}$ versus $\frac{1}{3}$

Same

- *same numerator*
- *less than 1/2*

Different

- *different denominators*
- *different values*

2. $\frac{2}{6}$ versus $\frac{1}{3}$

Same   Different

3. $\frac{4}{3}$ versus $\frac{2}{3}$

Same   Different

4.  versus

Same   Different

5. 0.15 versus 1.5

Same   Different

6. 2.4 x 0.3 versus 0.24 x 0.3

Same   Different

> > > > > > > > > > > > **COMPLETING THE CONNECTION** < < < < < < < < < < < < <

Complete the following analogy so that the relationship between the second pair is the same as the relationship between the first pair. $\frac{4}{8} : \frac{1}{2}$ as $\frac{6}{8}$: _____

Geometry

For each pair, state at least one way in which the items are the same and at least one way in which the items are different. List as many similarities and differences as you can.

1. ☐ versus ▱

Same

- *four sides*
- *four corners (angles)*

Different

- *one is a rectangle*
- *one is a parallelogram*

2. ◺ versus ◿

Same

Different

3. ⁴△⁴/₄ versus ⁶☐⁶ (6 top, 6 bottom)

Same

Different

4. ⊦ versus ⊤

Same

Different

5. ⊟ versus ▽

Same

Different

6. ⁶△⁶/₃ versus ⁴△⁴/₅

Same

Different

> > > > > > > > > > > **COMPLETING THE CONNECTION** < < < < < < < < < < < <

Complete the following analogy so that the relationship between the second pair is the same as the relationship between the first pair. 5 : pentagon as 6 : _____

Measurement

For each pair, state at least one way in which the items are the same and at least one way in which the items are different. List as many similarities and differences as you can.

1. m versus yd

Same

- *units of length*

Different

- *m is metric and yd is customary*
- *m is longer*

2. kg versus km

Same

Different

3. $3\boxed{}_5$ versus $4\boxed{}_4$

Same

Different

4. $3\boxed{}_8$ versus $4\boxed{}_6$

Same

Different

5. 0°C versus 32°F

Same

Different

6. $2\boxed{}_{2}{}^{2}$ versus $1\boxed{}_{2}{}^{4}$

Same

Different

> > > > > > > > > > > > **COMPLETING THE CONNECTION** < < < < < < < < < < < < <

Complete the following analogy so that the relationship between the second pair is the same as the relationship between the first pair. length : meter as weight : _____

Same and Different

Patterns and Relationships

For each pair, state at least one way in which the items are the same and at least one way in which the items are different. List as many similarities and differences as you can.

1. 15, 20, 25, 30 . . . versus 15, 10, 5, 0, −5 . . .

Same
  - *each starts with 15*
  - *difference of 5 between terms*

Different
  - *one increases and one decreases*
  - *first one will never include negative numbers*

2. 3, 5, 7, 9 . . . versus 3, 6, 12, 24 . . .

Same   Different

3. 1221 versus 1212

Same   Different

4. □, □□, □□□ . . . versus •, •••, ••••• . . .

Same   Different

5. 1, 2, 3, 5, 8 . . . versus 1, 2, 2, 4, 8 . . .

Same   Different

6. ↑, →, ↓, ←, ↑, →, ↓, ← . . . versus 1 2 3 4 1 2 3 4 . . .

Same   Different

> > > > > > > > > > > **COMPLETING THE CONNECTION** < < < < < < < < < < <

Complete the following analogy so that the relationship between the second pair is the same as the relationship between the first pair. 5, 10, 15, 20 : addition as 3, 6, 12, 24 : _____

Section 5

Example to Fit the Condition

Introduction

The **Example to Fit the Condition** activity format asks students to demonstrate understanding of concepts, relationships, or conditions. To show their understanding students are asked to list, write, draw, find, or show specified items.

The activity is open-ended, therefore student responses will vary. As students discuss their responses, it is critical that they make certain that each response does in fact fit the condition. As classroom responses are shared, students should communicate the properties and attributes that are critical to the question at hand.

Sample Exercises

For each statement, provide an example, diagram, number, expression, or written response to meet the given condition(s).

1. List two pairs of fractions whose sum is less than 1.

$$\frac{1}{8}, \frac{5}{8}$$

$$\frac{1}{4}, \frac{1}{3}$$

2.   Draw two triangles with perimeters of 12.

Other pairs of answers are possible for both questions.

In the Completing the Connection section, students are asked to state the concept represented by an illustration, or visual definition. The illustration may represent specific terms, relationships, or properties within the given cluster. For example, in the Geometry section, given the following illustration, students would be expected to indicate that it represents the definition of a rectangle.

Numeration and Number Sense

For each statement, provide a number or numbers to meet the given conditions.

1. Write the largest 3-digit number possible using the digits 2, 1, 8, and 6. No digit may be used more than once.
   862

2. Write the smallest 3-digit number possible using the digits 4, 9, 7, and 3. No digit may be used more than once.

3. Write the largest 3-digit number in which all the digits are different.

4. Write a number in which the hundreds digit is one more than the tens digit, and the tens digit is one more than the ones digit.

5. Write 3 numbers so that the first is 100 more than the second, and the second is 50 more than the third.

6. Write 3 numbers that are all multiples of 4 and multiples of 6.

7. Write the largest whole number that when rounded to the tens place rounds to 40.

8. Write the smallest whole number that when rounded to the tens place rounds to 80.

> > > > > > > > > > > **COMPLETING THE CONNECTION** < < < < < < < < < < < <

Identify the concept represented by the illustration.

Example to Fit the Condition   37

Operations

For each statement, provide a number or numbers to meet the given conditions.

1. List 3 numbers whose sum is between 100 and 200.
    51, 52, 53

2. List 2 numbers whose difference is less than 100.

3. List 2 numbers whose sum is greater than 1000 and whose difference is less than 150.

4. List 2 numbers whose product is between 400 and 600.

5. List 3 numbers that when divided by 5 each have a remainder of 1.

6. Find a number that when divided by either 2, 3, or 5 has a remainder of 1.

7. List 2 numbers whose sum is a palindrome.

8. Find 3 numbers whose average is 50.

> > > > > > > > > > > > **COMPLETING THE CONNECTION** < < < < < < < < < < < < <

Identify the concept represented by the illustration.

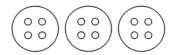

Fractions and Decimals

For each statement, provide a number or numbers to meet the given conditions.

1. List 2 fractions greater than 1.

$\frac{5}{3}, \frac{8}{5}$

2. List 3 fractions between $\frac{1}{4}$ and $\frac{1}{2}$.

3. List 3 decimals between 0.5 and 1.

4. Write the smallest decimal possible using all the digits 0, 5, and 4. No digit may be used more than once.

5. List 2 decimals that when rounded to nearest hundredth round to 0.57.

6. List 2 pairs of fractions that each have a sum greater than 1.

7. List 2 pairs of fractions that each have a product less than $\frac{1}{2}$.

8. List 2 pairs of fractions that each have a quotient of 1.

> > > > > > > > > > > > **COMPLETING THE CONNECTION** < < < < < < < < < < < < <

Identify the concept represented by the illustration.

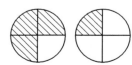

Geometry

For each statement, provide an example or diagram to meet the given condition.

1. Draw a quadrilateral that is neither a square nor a rectangle.

2. Draw a triangle that contains an obtuse angle.

3. Draw 2 triangles that are congruent.

4. Draw a quadrilateral with 1 pair of parallel sides.

5. Draw a pentagon with 2 right angles.

6. Draw 2 figures that are the same shape but not the same size.

7. Draw a figure that has at least 2 lines of symmetry.

8. Draw 2 solid figures with 6 faces each.

> > > > > > > > > > > > **COMPLETING THE CONNECTION** < < < < < < < < < < < < <

Identify the concept represented by the illustration.

Measurement

For each statement, provide an example, diagram, number, expression, or written response to meet the given condition.

1. Draw a rectangle with a perimeter of 16 units.

2. Draw a square with an area of 9 square units.

3. Find 3 classroom items that are longer than 1 meter.

4. Show how to represent 54¢ using 8 coins.

5. Show how to represent 65 items using dozens and units.

6. Draw a quadrilateral with an area of 6 square units and a perimeter of 10 units.

7. Draw a figure with a different shape but the same perimeter as the figure below.

8. Draw 2 solid figures that each have a volume of 24 cubic units.

> > > > > > > > > > > > **COMPLETING THE CONNECTION** < < < < < < < < < < < <

Identify the concept represented by the illustration.

$3 + 5 + 4 + 6$

Patterns and Relationships

For each statement, provide an example, diagram, number, expression, or written response to meet the given condition.

1. Write a sequence of even numbers containing 12 terms.

   20, 22, 24, 26, 28, 30, 32, 34, 36, 38, 40, 42

2. Write a sequence of 12 numbers in decreasing order.

3. Write a sequence of 12 fractions equivalent to $\frac{1}{2}$.

4. Write a sequence of 12 multiples of 6.

5. Write a sequence of 12 numbers in which the difference between the terms is 7.

6. Write a pattern of 12 terms made up an equal number of red, orange, and blue terms.

7. Write a sequence of odd multiples of 8.

8. Write a sequence of 3-digit palindromes between 100 and 200.

> > > > > > > > > > > **COMPLETING THE CONNECTION** < < < < < < < < < < < <

Identify the concept represented by the illustration.

Section 6

Problem Solving Revisited

Introduction

The **Problem Solving Revisited** activities are a potpourri of exercises that focus on skills related to solving multistep word problems. These exercises focus on strategies to help students become confident in dealing with this aspect of problem solving. The strategies depend on students' abilities to communicate ideas in a sequential fashion. The section contains six different exercise sets: Darts, What Operations?, First Things First, Common Thread, Help Me Pose a Problem, and One Step to Multistep.

Sample Exercises

Darts: Students write multistep expressions to describe dartboard scores as indicated in each diagram. Encourage students to create word problems illustrated by each diagram:

Example:

(4 x 10) + 8 Bill has 4 packages of 10 pencils and 8 loose pencils. How many pencils does he have in all?

What Operations?: Students indicate the sequence of operations required to total a group of prices. The objective of both the Darts and the What Operations? activities is to explore multistep situations, not to find solutions.

Example:

Items	Expression	Operations
$6.00, $6.00, $6.00, $4.50, $4.50, $4.50, $4.50	*(3 x $6.00) + (4 x $4.50)*	*multiplication, multiplication, addition*

First Things First: Students identify only the first step in the solution process for a multistep word problem. As a subsequent activity, students could be asked to solve the actual problem, but analyzing the first step is the focus here. Have students discuss why the step they indicate is reasonable as a first step in the solution process.

Example: Elizabeth purchased 3 containers of juice at $0.79 each. How much change did she receive from $5.00?

The first step is $.79 x 3

Common Thread: Students write expressions to solve the given word problems, and then identify the situation that is common to all the problems. In these examples the common thread is that both involve multiplication followed by subtraction.

Example 1: Maria saved $5.45 a week for 3 weeks, and then lost a quarter at school. How much money did she have left?

(3 x 5.45) – 0.25

Example 2: From a sheet of 100 stamps, 4 rows of 10 stamps are removed. How many stamps remain?

100 – (4 x 10)

Help Me Pose a Problem: Students provide missing information that will allow a standard problem to be solved. The underlying assumption is that students will increase their ability to solve and discuss a variety of standard problems as they identify missing information.

Example: Sally bought 5 greeting cards at $1.25 each. How much change did she receive?

Sally paid with a $10.00 bill.

One Step to Multistep: Students create word problems related to a given set of data. They change a one-step problem into a two-step problem, and then write a three-step problem. The objective is for students to develop a better understanding of the distinction between one-step problems and multistep problems.

Example: Chan purchased 3 pens at $1.19 each. How much did he spend? Add to your problem to make it a two-step problem.

Chan purchased 3 pens at $1.19 each. How much change did he receive from $10.00?

In the Completing the Connection activities, students create examples similar to the ones presented on the page. For instance, after the Common Thread activity, students write another problem that would be solved using the same solution sequence as the problems on the page. Have students share their original examples in a small-group or class discussion.

<•><•><•><•><•><•><•><•><•><•><•><•><•><•><•><•><•><•><•>

Darts

Write a multistep expression for each situation. Be prepared to discuss your answer.

1. $(2 \times 5) + (8 + 4)$

2.

3.

4.

5.

6.

> > > > > > > > > > > > **COMPLETING THE CONNECTION** < < < < < < < < < < < <

Write a word problem to go with each
diagram and multistep expression above.

What Operations?

For each exercise, write an expression in mathematical terms to find the total for each set of items. Write the sequence of operations needed to find the total. For exercises 7 and 8, reverse the process.

Items	Expression	Operation(s)
1. $2.98, $3.54, $3.54	2.98 + (2 x 3.54)	*multiplication and addition*
2. $2, $2, $2, $2		
3. $4, $4, $4, $4, $9		
4. $4, $4, $4, $5, $5, $5		
5. 16 items at $3 each		
6. 5 items at $3 each and 10 items at $2 each		
7. _____ items selling at _____ each	10 x $6	
8. _____ items selling at _____ and _____ items selling at _____	(10 x $4) + $8	

> > > > > > > > > > > > **COMPLETING THE CONNECTION** < < < < < < < < < < < < <

List items that could be totaled using multiplication, multiplication, multiplication, and addition.

First Things First

For each of the following multistep problems, show the first step in the solution process. Be prepared to discuss why your choice is a reasonable first step in finding the solution.

1. Janet bought a notebook for $2.95 and 4 pens at $1.09 each. How much did she spend?

   Find the cost of the pens by multiplying 4 x $1.09.

2. How much change would you receive from $20.00 if you bought 7 pairs of socks at $2.95 a pair?

3. You and a friend earned $10.50 mowing a lawn. You shared the money equally. You spent $1.50 of your money. How much money do you have left?

4. A patrol group of 9 scouts is chosen from a group of 63 scouts. The rest of the scouts are divided into work groups of 6. How many work groups are there?

5. The juice bar sold 14 glasses of apple juice, 37 glasses of orange juice, and 21 glasses of grape juice. Each glass holds 8 ounces. How many ounces of juice did the juice bar sell altogether?

6. Pat's math grades are 83, 79, 80, 82, and 86. What is Pat's average in math?

> > > > > > > > > > > **COMPLETING THE CONNECTION** < < < < < < < < < < < <

Write a multistep word problem for a friend to solve in
which the first step in the solution requires multiplication.

Common Thread

For each problem, write an expression to find the solution. Compare the written expressions to find a pattern.

1. If you have 9 individual pencils and 10 packages of pencils with 12 pencils in each package, what is your total number of pencils?

    (10 x 12) + 9

2. You have 6 loose postage stamps and a rectangular sheet of postage stamps. Your sheet of stamps has 10 rows with 5 in each row. What is the total number of stamps?

3. You have 3 quarters and 4 pennies in your pocket. How much money do you have in all?

4. In a refrigerator, you have 5 eggs and also 2 dozen eggs. What is the total number of eggs in the refrigerator?

5. An auditorium is set up with 20 rows of chairs. Each row has 16 seats. In addition, there are 15 extra chairs in various locations within the auditorium. What is the maximum number of children to be seated in the auditorium?

6. If you are given that the area of the triangle pictured is 20 square units, what is the area of the entire figure pictured?

> > > > > > > > > > > > **COMPLETING THE CONNECTION** < < < < < < < < < < < <

Write a problem that is solved using the same solution
sequence as the problems on this page.

Help Me Pose a Problem

Write a complete sentence to provide the additional information needed to solve each problem. Answers may vary. (You do not have to give the answer to the problem.)

1. Chan bought 2 cassette tapes. Each tape cost $5.96. How much change did he receive?
   Chan gave the clerk $20.00.

2. Victor bought 1 notebook and 4 pens for a total cost of $3.50. How much did the notebook cost?

3. The price of a shirt was decreased $15. What was the new price of the shirt?

4. Bobby has $3.75 in nickels, dimes, and quarters. He has more nickels than dimes. How many quarters does he have?

5. Irene wants to fence in her garden. The width of her garden is 6 feet. How many feet of fence does she need in all?

6. There are 184 students going on a field trip. How many buses are needed for the trip?

> > > > > > > > > > > **COMPLETING THE CONNECTION** < < < < < < < < < < < <

Write an incomplete problem like those in the activity above. Have a partner
provide the needed information and use it to solve the problem.

One Step to Multistep

Use the data given below to write problems as directed.

```
                        School Store
Notebook   $1.25      Assignment Pad    $.50
Pen        $ .35      Marker            $.60
Pencil     $ .20      Poster Paper      $.20
Eraser     $ .15      Ruler             $.25
```

1. Write a one-step problem.

   How much would you pay for 5 pencils?

2. Add to your problem to make it a two-step problem.

3. Show a different way to add to your one-step problem from number 1 to make it a two-step problem.

4. Write another two-step problem.

5. Show how you can change your two-step problem from number 4 to make it a little different.

6. Write a three-step problem.

> > > > > > > > > > > **COMPLETING THE CONNECTION** < < < < < < < < < < <

Write a problem that can be solved using multiplication and subtraction.

Answer Section

Section I: Which One Doesn't Belong?

Page 5 (Numeration and Number Sense):
2. A, the others are all in the thirties decade; C, the others are even; D, the others are dates on the calendar. 3. D, the others are multiples of 4. 4. C, the others are equivalent to 54. 5. B, the others are whole-number places. 6. A, the others are increasing sequences of consecutive numbers. 7. B, the others are less than 100. 8. D, the others round to 80.

Page 6 (Operations):
2. C, the others equal 8. 3. C, the others equal 100. 4. D, the other sums are approximately 100. 5. D, the others differ by 10. 6. C, the others have differences of about 100. 7. D, the others are expressions for 625 divided by 25. 8. A, the others equal 140.

Page 7 (Fractions and Decimals):
2. C, the others are equal to 1/2. 3. B, the others can be reduced. 4. D, the others are equivalent to 1/2. 5. D, the others are equivalent to 1/2 of a basic unit. 6. A, the others are improper fractions. 7. B, the other pairs add to 1. 8. C, the others are greater than 1 1/2.

Page 8 (Geometry):
2. D, the others are three-dimensional figures. 3. C, the others are right triangles. 4. A, the others are acute angles. 5. B, the other lines will intersect. 6. C, the others are congruent figures. 7. B, the others have line symmetry. 8. B, the others are reflections of the letter.

Page 9 (Measurement):
2. D, the others are measures of time. 3. D, the others are units of capacity. 4. B, the others are months of 31 days. 5. A, the other temperatures are above freezing. 6. D, the others are equivalent to 18". 7. B, the other perimeters are equal to 12. 8. B, the other areas are equal to 36.

Page 10 (Patterns and Relationships):
2. D, the others are sequences formed by adding 2. 3. A, the others are sequences formed by subtracting 3. 4. D, the others are sequences formed by adding 10. 5. B, the others are palindromes. 6. C, the others are palindromes. 7. A, the others have numerators and denominators that differ by 2. 8. B, the others have hundredths places that are twice the tenths place.

Section 2: How Do You Know That?

Page 13 (Numeration and Number Sense):
(Answers may vary.)
2. 5 tens is more than 3 tens. 3. The 4 is in the hundreds place and should be in the thousands place. 4. 46 is one more than 45 and one less than 47. 5. 14 ones can be

53

regrouped to 1 ten and 4 ones. 1 ten and 4 ones plus 4 tens is 54. **6.** Each of the 4 addends round to 100, giving an estimate of 400. **7.** When 42 is divided by 4 you get a remainder. **8.** If a number ends in anything but 5 or 0 when you divide by 5 you get a remainder.

Page 14 (Operations):
2. Multiplication is repeated addition of the same number a given number of times. 3 x 5 means add 5 three times. **3.** If you take 17 away from 17 you get 0. 25 is more than 17, therefore, the difference must be less than 0. **4.** 710 – 590 is greater than 0, but 590 – 710 is less than 0. **5.** 235 is evenly divisible by 5. Since 236 is the next number, the remainder would be 1. **6.** Since 34 x 4 is not equal to 1216, 34 is not the quotient. **7.** 40 x 30 is equal to 1200, and 50 x 30 is equal to 1500. Since 45 x 32 is between these two products, the product is between 1200 and 1500. **8.** The average cannot be greater than the largest number in the set.

Page 15 (Fractions and Decimals):
2. If fractions have the same numerator the larger the denominator the smaller the fraction. Since 5 is greater than 4, 1/5 is less than 1/4. **3.** 7/6 is an improper fraction, therefore it is greater than 1. **4.** Since 2/3 is greater than 1/2 and 2 + 3 is equal to 5, 2 1/2 + 3 2/3 is greater than 6. **5.** 16 and 25 share no common factors, therefore 16/25 cannot be reduced. **6.** Since 0.7 is greater than 0.5 and 0.5 + 0.5 is equal to 1, 0.5 + 0.7 is greater than 1. **7.** 4 tenths is greater than no tenths, hence 0.045 is less than 0.405. **8.** Since 2/5 is less than 1 and 2.5 is greater than 1, 2/5 is not equal to 2.5.

Page 16 (Geometry):
2. A square, like a rectangle, has opposite sides equal and parallel, and all angles are right angles. **3.** < ABC is larger than a right angle, and acute angles are less than right angles. **4.** To be congruent, figures must have the same size and shape. Rectangles can be different sizes. **5.** Triangle ABC and triangle DEF are exactly the same size and shape. **6.** If a horizontal line is drawn through the middle of the E, the top and bottom portions are identical. **7.** The letter has two changes in orientation, which requires two reflections. **8.** Since all the faces of a cube are squares, you cannot get a circular imprint.

Page 17 (Measurement):
2. If a rectangle has dimensions 3 by 5 the perimeter is 16. If the dimensions are doubled to 6 by 10 the perimeter becomes twice as big, 32. **3.** If a rectangle has dimensions 3 by 5, the area is 15. If the dimensions are doubled to 6 by 10, the area becomes 60, 4 times as large. **4.** 2 quarters, 1 dime, 2 nickels is equivalent to 70 cents. 7 dimes are also equivalent to 70 cents. **5.** Since each week contains 7 days, the next Saturday will be March 21 and March 22 will be Sunday. **6.** One meter equals 100 cm, therefore 4 meters equals 400 cm. **7.** 48 inches equal 4 feet, which is greater than 3 feet 6 inches; 3 feet 6 inches equals 42 inches, which is less than 48 inches. **8.** The maximum number of days a month can contain is 31. If the first is on a Monday, then the successive Mondays are 1, 8, 15, 22, 29. The last day of the month would be a Wednesday.

Page 18 (Patterns and Relationships):
2. Each term is equal to three times the number of its place. So the tenth term is 3 x 10, or 30. **3.** The sequence is formed by the polygons classified by number of sides. The hexagon has 6 sides, so the next figure would have to be a heptagon, which has 7 sides. **4.** The sequence is fractions equivalent to 2/3, and 9/12 is not equivalent to 2/3. **5.** O occurs in every third place. Since 20 is not divisible by 3, O cannot be in the 20th place. **6.** 1011 written backwards is 1101, which is not the same as 1011. **7.** The sequence is decreasing by 5, and 5 less than 0

is a negative number. **8.** Each term is built by an odd number of tiles. Hence the 15th term must be odd also.

Section 3: What If?

Page 21 (Numeration and Number Sense):
2. An even number results. **3.** The number is 3142. **4.** 10,000 bundles are needed. **5.** 43 is not divisible by 3 and is therefore not included. **6.** The peanuts can be shared by 1, 2, 3, 4, 6, or 9 people. **7.** 9654 is the largest. **8.** 347 is the largest.

Page 22 (Operations):
2. The sum is doubled. **3.** The difference stays the same. **4.** The product is 4 times greater. **5.** The product stays the same. **6.** The quotient stays the same. **7.** The quotient is 4 times larger. **8.** The product increases.

Page 23 (Fractions and Decimals):
2. The fraction stays the same. **3.** The value of the fraction decreases. **4.** The value of the fraction is greater than 1. **5.** The value of the fraction increases. **6.** The value of the fraction increases. **7.** The value decreases ten times. **8.** The value increases one hundred times.

Page 24 (Geometry):
2. Two acute acute angles are formed. **3.** A rectangle is formed. **4.** Rotate the card 90° clockwise. **5.** The figure has line symmetry. **6.** A cylinder is formed. **7.** A rectangle is formed. **8.** The shape is a pyramid.

Page 25 (Measurement):
2. The area becomes four times greater. **3.** The area stays the same. **4.** The volume becomes 8 times greater. **5.** The month has 28 days. **6.** New Year's Eve will be on Friday. **7.** The temperature will be 37°F. **8.** It is 9:59.

Page 26 (Patterns and Relationships):
2. The terms are 15, 25, 40, 65, 105. **3.** The

term is green. **4.** The direction of the arrow is ← . **5.** Nothing; the terms would still differ from each other by 3. **6.** The sum is 210. **7.** Five tiles are needed. **8.** The terms are 5, 0, −5, −10, and −15.

Section 4: Same and Different

Page 29 (Numeration and Number Sense): (Answers will vary.)
2. *Same*: both are even numbers; both are multiples of 3, 4, 6, 12; *Different:* number of ones and tens, 24 is divisible by 8, 36 is divisible by 9 and 18. **3.** *Same:* number of tens, both round to 20; *Different:* one number is odd, one is even; 18 is divisible by 3 and 6; 19 is prime. **4.** *Same:* both are powers of ten, both are written as 1 followed by zeros, both are even numbers; *Different:* one is 1000 times larger, number of digits in each number. **5.** *Same:* same value; *Different:* one has less than 10 ones. **6.** *Same:* same value; *Different:* one is written as a Roman numeral.

Page 30 (Operations):
2. *Same:* both have two addends, both sums are approximately 500; *Different:* one sum is greater than 500, one sum is odd, one is even. **3.** *Same:* same numbers used in the problems; *Different:* one is addition, one is subtraction. **4.** *Same:* same divisor; *Different:* different dividends, one quotient is ten times the other. **5.** *Same:* both are a 2-digit number divided by a 1-digit number, both have remainders of 3, both have quotients of 6 R 3; *Different:* different divisor, different dividend. **6.** *Same:* both have an average of 20, both have numbers that are multiples of 10; *Different:* number of numbers being averaged.

Page 31 (Fractions and Decimal):
2. *Same:* both equal 1/3; *Different:* one is not in lowest terms, different numerators and denominators. **3.** *Same:* same denominator, numerators are even numbers; *Different:* one

has value greater than 1, different numerators. **4.** *Same:* both equal 1/2 of whole; *Different:* differently shaped regions of whole. **5.** *Same:* same digits, both are decimals; *Different:* values are different, one is greater than 1, one is ten times greater than the other. **6.** *Same:* digits, one factor in each is 0.3, last digit of the product is 2. *Different:* one product is ten times the other, number of decimal places in problem.

Page 32 (Geometry):
2. *Same:* both are triangles, both are right triangles; *Different:* one is larger. **3.** *Same:* both are equilateral figures, dimensions are even numbers; *Different:* perimeters, shapes, number of sides. **4.** *Same:* both are letters of alphabet, both have lines of symmetry; *Different:* "T" has vertical symmetry, "E" has horizontal symmetry. **5.** *Same:* both are 3-dimensional shapes, both have circular bases; *Different:* one is a cylinder, one is a cone, they have different volumes. **6.** *Same:* both are triangles, both are isosceles triangles; *Different:* angle measures, dimensions, perimeter.

Page 33 (Measurement):
2. *Same:* both are metric units, both are 1000 times the basic unit; *Different:* one is a unit of weight, one is a unit of length. **3.** *Same:* perimeter, both are rectangles; *Different:* one is a square, one has greater area. **4.** *Same:* both are rectangles, same area; *Different:* perimeter. **5.** *Same:* both are freezing points; *Different:* temperature scales. **6.** *Same:* volume, both are rectangular prisms; *Different:* one is a cube, one has all square faces.

Page 34 (Patterns and Relationships):
2. *Same:* lead term; *Different:* one adds 2 to generate next term, one multiplies previous term by 2 for next term, one is all odd numbers. **3.** *Same:* digits, number of thousands and hundreds; *Different:* one is a palindrome; one is odd, one is even. **4.** *Same:* both are sequences made up of geometric shapes,

both start with one shape; *Different:* one is triangular, one is square. **5.** *Same:* first two terms; *Different:* one is generated by taking the sum of the two previous terms, one is generated by taking the product of the two previous terms. **6.** *Same:* both are ABCD patterns; *Different:* one is numbers, one is arrows.

Section 5: Example to Fit the Condition

Page 37 (Numeration and Number Sense): (Answers may vary.)
2. 347 **3.** 987 **4.** 543 (etc.) **5.** 160, 60, 10 **6.** 12, 24, 36 **7.** 44 **8.** 75

Page 38 (Operations):
2. 543, 473 **3.** 600, 500 **4.** 20 x 25 **5.** 16, 26, 31 **6.** 31 **7.** 110, 11 **8.** 40, 50, 60

Page 39 (Fractions and Decimals):
2. 1/3, 3/10, 2/5 **3.** 0.6, 0.75, 0.9 **4.** 0.045 **5.** 0.574, 0.569 **6.** 3/5, 4/5; 2/3, 1/2 **7.** 1/3, 1/4; 2/3, 1/2 **8.** 4/5, 4/5; 3/8, 3/8

Page 40 (Geometry):

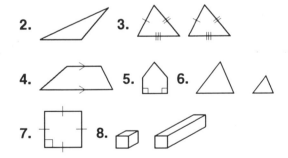

Page 41 (Measurement):

2. **3.** Answers may vary. **4.** 1 quarter, 1 nickel, 2 dimes, 4 pennies **5.** 5 dozen, 5 units **6.** **7.**

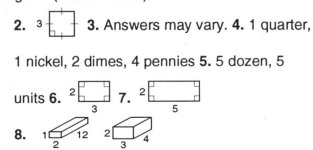

Page 42 (Patterns and Relationships):
(Answers may vary.)
   2. 24, 22, 20, 18, 16, 14, 12, 10, 8, 6, 4, 2.
   3. 2/4, 3/6, 4/8, 5/10, 6/12, 7/14, 8/16, 9/18,
   10/20, 11/22, 12/24, 13/26. **4.** 0, 6, 12, 18, 24,
   30, 36, 42, 48, 54, 60, 66. **5.** 1, 8, 15, 22, 29,
   36, 43, 50, 57, 64, 71, 78. **6.** red, orange, blue,
   red, orange, blue, red, orange, blue, red,
   orange, blue. **7.** not possible; all whole-number
   multiples of 8 are even. **8.** 101, 111, 121, 131,
   141, 151, 161, 171, 181, 191

Section 6: Problem Solving Revisited

Page 46 (Darts):
   2. 10 + (5 x 8) + 4 **3.** (3 x 5) + (2 x 10)
   4. (4 x 5) + (5 x 4) **5.** (6 x 5) + (7 x 4) **6.** (3 x 5)
   + (5 x 10) + (6 x 4) + (5 x 8)

Page 47 (What Operations?):
   2. 4 x $2, multiplication **3.** 4 x $4 + $9, multipli-
   cation and addition **4.** 3 x $4 + 3 x $5,
   multiplication, multiplication, addition **5.** 16 x
   $3, multiplication **6.** 5 x $3 + 10 x $2, multipli-
   cation, multiplication, addition **7.** 10, $6,
   multiplication **8.** 10 @ $4, 1 @ $8 multiplication and addition

Page 48 (First Things First):
   2. Find the total cost of the socks by multiplying
   7 x $2.95. **3.** Divide the $10.50 by 2 to find
   each share. **4.** Subtract 9 from 63 to find the
   number of scouts to be placed in groups.
   5. Add 14, 37, and 21 to find the total number
   of glasses sold. **6.** Add the scores 83, 79, 80,
   82, and 86 to find the total of the 5 tests.

Page 49 (Common Thread):
   2. (10 x 5) + 6 **3.** (3 x $.25) + $.04 **4.** (2 x 12) +
   5 **5.** (20 x 16) + 15 **6.** (4 x 10) + 20. All solutions involve multiplication followed by
   addition.

Page 50 (Help Me Pose a Problem):
(Answers may vary.)
   2. A pen costs $0.50 **3.** The original price of
   the shirt is $45. **4.** The nickels and dimes add
   up to $1.25 **5.** The garden is twice as long as it
   is wide. **6.** Each bus seats 45 people.

Page 51 (One Step to Multistep):
(Answers may vary.)
   2. What is your change from $10 if you buy
   five pencils? **3.** How much would you pay for
   five pencils and a notebook? **4.** If you buy two
   notebooks, what is your change from $5.00?
   5. If you buy two notebooks and a marker,
   what is your change from $5.00? **6.** If you
   have $3, will you have enough money to buy
   four markers and one assignment pad?